## Responses to Gardens and Caves

Poetry is essentially and at its core, a distillation of emotions and experiences; that which Wordsworth referred to as the "spontaneous overflow of powerful emotions recollected in tranquility."

This is clearly true and evident in the poems of Emmanuel Uweru Okoh collected under the title, *Gardens and Caves.*

In the evocative, reflective and exhilarating lines that populate the pages of his debut collection, Okoh is like a sponge that soaks up incidents, emotions, actions and every manner of experience. His poems speak to our common humanity by chronicling our joys and pains, our flights and awkward stumbles, and all else that makes us who we are.

In language that is both flagellating and soothing, he mines the depths of our reality but there is always hope despite the gloom as he writes:

But if lucky, you'll meet a few
Good ones; dedicated and straight
But only few, very few.

This is eloquent poetry for our uncertain times!
— **Toni Kan**, Poet and Novelist.

Poetry still walks and talks among the living — *Gardens and Caves* proves this much. Emmanuel writes poems his readers can own; good poetry. Here is a voice that will linger for a long, long time.
— **Efe Paul Azino**, Poet and Social Critic

Emmanuel Uweru Okoh is a poet whose sensibilities are attuned to Nature, her elements, her cycles and the voices of her human children. *Gardens and Caves* is a celebration of Courage and Growth. This collection is a celebration of fearlessness, consciousness and remarkable aesthetics.

— **Saraba Magazine**

Gardens and Caves, two words contrary to each other! Poetic image emerges from contrasts. When you enter a garden, you see flowers in beautiful colours. Correspondingly, it is bats that you come face to face with when you go into a cave. They both have cries. A good poet must hear cries of blossoms at the moment they blow up. Emmanuel Uweru Okoh writes the cries out of *Gardens and Caves.*

— **İlyas Tunç**, Turkish Poet, Author and Translator.

# GARDENS
### AND
# CAVES

# GARDENS
## AND
# CAVES

◆◆◆◆◆◆◆◆◆◆◆◆◆◆◆◆◆◆◆◆◆◆◆◆◆◆◆

## POEMS BY
## EMMANUEL UWERU OKOH

SUNBIRD BOOKS
LAGOS, NIGERIA

First published in Nigeria in 2012 by Sunbird Books
An imprint of Sunbird African Media
and
Mace Associates Limited
4 Odunukan Avenue
Oregun, Ikeja, Lagos, Nigeria
Tel: 234-1-734-6765
Mobile: 234-706-3819-929
Email: sunbirdbooks@gmail.com
www.sunbird.com.ng

© 2012 Emmanuel Uweru Okoh

A catalogue record of this book is available from the National Library of Nigeria.

ISBN: 978-978-8033-15-8

Cover art and illustrations by Paul Akpokodje
Book design by Olatunde Ashaolu
Author's photograph by Ewere Iwelu

# CONTENTS

## WHISPERS OF NATURE

## LIVING AND HEREAFTER

## HAIKU

# DEDICATION

*To the joy of family love and true friendship (if you find one)*
*And to **You**, for believing in the noble art of writing*

# INTRODUCTION

Each section in this poetry collection, Gardens and Caves presents a stepping stone in the circle of life, as it strings together nature appreciation, inspiration, political power play and family life. The collection concludes with the famed Haiku poetry of the Japanese.

# ****CIRCLE OF INSPIRATION****

## SETTING FORTH

Just when you thought of moving,
your feet grew cold and stiff.
You had the will, but the means said no,
distorting your focus.
Those voices didn't help.
Voices telling you to sit and stare.
Those whispers held you spellbound;
telling you:
"you can't"
"wait a little more"
"you're too old"
"forget it"
"you were born this way"
"it is your fate"

But can you feel the clash in those
voices?
It is war within. And you will win.
No stories, excuses. No tears.
Listen to that other voice;
The calm one; serene but steadfast
That is you. The will that is whole
That is all you need for this journey.
You can set forth.

# SONG OF THE ARCHITECT

I had the dream of Milan's Palazzo Lombardia
And Canada's Absolute Towers.
To create such and more.
Then the Taj Mahal would seem dead.

Sitting out on a Harmattan morning
I had my brain and drawing board.
The breeze and chilly hugs
Accompanied by a mug of coffee

A masterpiece was sure
Before the ants towed in line
In firm order; prudent
Building without drawing

Then I thought about
The structure of the anthill; ingenuous
The unseen columns, the stairs
Then I stooped for the ant's tutelage.

## SIXTH REALM

The night denied the day and cursed light.
But never forget the tale of the fair king:
Triumphant in all, but one; death

Who, then are you to move?
Who sanctioned your progress?
Who willed your will?

But, on this path, they trudged
Frail and bowed limbs
Sketched on virgin lands
If you will, tighten those bone pieces
With loose tendrils – We have a long way.

But, distance is vague, meaningless in this quest.
In this new realm, time is futile:
We breathe in endless sequence.

# A PATH FOR TEN

How, that November morning, we set out
    amidst mist and dew. A few clenched fists, protecting
        us from nature's bite. On and on, we trudged on the snaky

farm path. Slowly we weaved through these shrubs and
    shrunken earth. Our view from the flying metal: ten men
        on the back of an endless python; like a spooky old rail

I see you now, then I don't in a while; switch twitch
    like a drunken clock, telling lies of time and unsolicited
        predictions.  Hold on to the present view, and follow your

front man. If we make this journey, we'll seek the face of
    the god of snaky paths - in rendition of gratitude.  If one man
        goes down, we'll have a mutiny on the gods of snaky paths

## KALAKUTA VOICE
*(For Fela Anikulapo Kuti)*

Deeper in prophecy the voice waxed
Channeling truth beyond imagination
Afro-truth allergic to incarceration

Kalakuta needed to breathe
For her song within to be free,
That cave of creative madness

The heart of Kalakuta remains
Within that cave. Baba Olufela told me,
The unborn poet. It is the Afro-truth

Futile will be a billion canons,
Mere pelts against Kalakuta's walls
A grand rebirth. Kalakuta is alive!

# THE MARATHON
*(for Usain  St. Leo Bolt)*

With the starting shot, I sprang
Heels over shoulders.
This race, this pace
Pushing ahead beyond the gasps.
This chant, this song in my head
Keeps me going. Keeps me in lane.
Throbbing heart. Pulse in sync.

I am alone in this race
I beat me
My last record, I must break
The troubles of defeat I forsake
My mind on the finish line
The prize, definitely mine.

# WHEN I SING…

I will sing today,
The song of tomorrow
Clad in nude notes.
Claps of thunder and earthly tugs,
Render beats and rhythm.

When I sing, tomorrow
Becomes today, and uncertainty
Bows in eternal submission
Knees kissing the earth,
Tongue kissing dust.

I will sing today,
That song of awakened rivers
With a voice of virile timbre,
Pitch of sonority
And soothing words

When you hear me,
Wipe those tears of mercury
And lost hope.
Clink the victorious glasses
And sip in unison

# JUMOKE

*Jumoke* scraped all of it; hair and scalp. She needed nothing for this new journey of solitude. She whispered to the *Iroko*: "Be my man, I know you are strong enough". When morning came, the canary called her name-thrice-trying to make the fourth call but fought hard to stop. The birds brought grains in bits, till a fistful made a meal. She gulped from an upturned pod. Facial gullies led streams of salt down her cheeks.

Nails dripped blood
Sun dried blood

Red scales fell to earth
And met the stream of
Her salt.

She *died*.
And lived-once more: a new *Jumoke*.

# FOR QUA IBOE

Grand birth in '87
Stringing voices of
Ibibio through Eket

Bearing Amazons of famed glory-
Glory shared with sister Calabar
Your glory berths

*"For Qua Iboe" was shortlisted for the 2012 Akwa Ibom State Silver Jubilee poetry contest*

## BEFORE MORNING

Before morning, breathe in…
Breathe in this darkness and use this still
Dark air. There is power within these colours
You can't touch; the strength of your fathers
Reverberates in whirling motions. Step into
This ring of rare time, nostrils, first then your
Eyes and ears. Before morning, nurture the thoughts
Of tomorrow and abort the knell of sad tales.
Make the day at night, for the night is the day.
Before morning, breathe out…

# VINDICATION

Though I bear these forced marks of crime,
The hallmark of innocence is etched on my heart.
Deep within these facial gullies are streams of Clearwater-
Signifying thoughts of mirror purity
And rushing beats of saintly sanctity

Again, you taunt me with burning spikes
And aged rusted cuffs
Leaving inflated lines on my burning sides
And playing deaf to my coughs

If only I could puncture the goggles of the gods
To see further than their palatial abodes
To see the fluctuating journey of these rods
On my tender spine. Nerves truncated in droves.

Though I bear these marks of cross reasoning.
I see traces of upturned death within these shores
Deep within the roaring ocean is a bed of calmness
Reflecting my true sanity
Displaying my purity.

# ANTIDOTE

A medicine man's death it was
A scenario of Solomon's wits end
He wished for a heart for problems to bear
Without remorse, we turned in shame
Who knows how?
And how, who knows what?
The antidote is in the air

# SARO WIWA'S WAITING WAR...

*(for Ken Saro Wiwa)*
My keen cry to Kenule: I, Fubara, of the disjointed
Fishnet and gaping boat, from the land of kernel
Back feeling and staggering heritage.
Of gasping fish and de-flowered flowers,
Of frowning waters and stunted stalks
I sit on a lonely log; One of the few remaining.
I write on Dutchman's Dollar paper.
It left the Howling Helicopter.
Black crude: my ink, my thin thighs: my table.
It's a stolen converse Kenule, so, listen.
I know you still hear truth.

Your ink bullets still hover in mid-mission,
Taking stolen rests on shrunken leaves and
Greased waters. The cruel antics of the goggled
General regenerates in bloody resonance,
Feeding the rusty rulers of our land.
We await the revolution of fish and oysters
From long years of petrol-logged breath
And bone splinters from Shell's shell.
Let the cry of prawns and lobsters
Aid my call to you Kenule, while my throat
Is lubricated by this crude I drink.

Bright glow from Dutch giant metal
Candles steal our nights, blasting insects that dare
Hover. Caked soot sits on my nasal paths.
I breathe with my ears; ears saturated with news of
Inverted justice, of blood soaked loots I loathe.

Hear these words Kenule. And berth those
Ink bullets of fourth estate fame and stencil
Romance. That short romance of eternal frenzy
And gothic engravings of your letters that die
Not from 'feeble' minds of Generals nor fumes
From Dutch industrial farts.

*"Saro Wiwa's Waiting War" was a nominee entry in the 2010 memorial essay contest for the late activist and writer, Ken Saro Wiwa. The poem was recited at the commemorative vigil for Saro Wiwa in Houston, Texas, USA.*

## STRANGE COLOURS

Faint flickering flashes on a cold night
Of colours unnamed. A beautiful 'colour-light'
Tango, slips through my blinds and takes its place
In my room. I watch from my bed of lonely pillows.
My pillows are time marks of fond memories.

Memories of you and I. Sweet scent of your fragrance
Caress cozy sheets, tormenting my olfactory sense,
Like the plagues of Egypt. Strange colours sit beside me
In perpetual comfort. These colours have your smile.
These colours have your touch. In these colours I see hope.

In these colours I touch my dreams. Dreams I thought I lost
When you walked away, like a marooned mum.
To Solitude Island. As you return in these strange colours;
We tie cords of passion. Never to despair and sigh
Strangers to pain and vicissitude

I shall welcome the carnival of dancing pallets and talking
Drums to herald your come-back. Let the Lion's roar
Still your hovering spirit. Let the maids serve these colours,
While *Enyi* stomps its feet for my triumph;
My triumph of repossessed glory.

Let the monkeys climb trees of happiness as they munch
A thousand fingers of banana. When the carnival is over,
*Okorie*, the village tailor will make a strange robe
Of strange colours, a robe of a million lights for this strange
Come-back. Glad is my heart, for *Adanne* is back!

# A CANDLE'S LIFE

Silent stick of flamed crown
With cerebral thread of torture
Your bright crown cuts your life
With unseen blazing blades

A Tower of Ivory to the ants
But, they dare not climb
For your crown is fierce.
Its fury knows no mercy.

Mama lights your crown each night
One, two or three; the more the
Merrier, as you illuminate our
Cocoon, corners and crevices.

Your short wax life,
Waves a wand of warmth as
I warm my cold palms
Above your crown

My blood is free like the Nile
But yours stops in mid trickle
As it departs the crown
And builds along your wall

A brief life of munificence
As selfless as Mother Theresa
With nothing to gain, and light to give
A candle's life

## UGBOH NTA

Earth's portion with a heart
I feel your agony of neglect-
Lonely when the
Household sets out for *ugboh ukwu*

She gets all the attention: A raffia hut
For company, and a hundred feet
To caress her rich back.  She knows
Our story: she hears it all; *ugboh ukwu*

Be consoled,
The mushrooms and okras are appreciated.
Those handy corn cobs and berry bunch too.
Petit piece of providence; *ugboh nta*.
When the season's charred, I'll sooth
Your mood with bright tales

# ****Political Equation****

## CRAZY DIALECTICS

This hate party at the hallowed chambers…
Who is the host?

Rants, Hisses, Curses and Smiles
Slaps, Kicks, Scratches and Hugs

A mad house full of crispy linen and scent
Of exclusive preserve
Dialectics for citizens whose houses are full
Of threadbare linen and foul smell

Go on; push your microphone button and release
A stream of falsehood:
Lies, lies, lies and just too few good.
The people tarry for change…
For the new order to come alive…
Say 'Aye' or 'Nay?'
We say 'Aye'

# FALSEHOOD

The invention of falsehood:
Must we shuttle this ring of monumental deceit?
Official anti-climax behind parliamentary desks and
Residential barricades; indications of backwardness

The convention of falsehood:
A million committees
A thousand panels of inquiry
Meetings in thin air

Products of falsehood:
Bare back children, yelling at hungry
Parents. Dysfunctional system pointing
The barrel at you, I and us.

# ARMY ARRANGEMENT

Just when we thought
The carnival was over
We heard stomps throughout
That made warriors quiver

The khaki boys ploughed and ripped forth
Tearing down all that peace could render
Gigantic loots. None questioned or fought
For if you did, your sojourn would be over

Atrocities tough as iron wrought
Our plight did less for a mind make over
Instead, incarcerations flowed forth
Including brave men of steel liver

But the struggle was weaved on thought
So on, and on and on victory rolled over
And just when the carnival music stopped
An *agbada*-wearing khaki boy took over

# CIVILIAN ARRANGEMENT

The party just started
All seated, pot bellied; loud laughs and fine wines

Deliberation sessions
Official proposals, lame in all ramifications; we are so selfish.

Projects of dreamland
Four, eight years. "Abeg give me more time"; tenure elongation

*Katakata* remedy
Bombings and all. "We shall look into it; Calm down my people."

## POLICE ARRANGEMENT

'Oya park well'
Imbroglio of stop and search.
Haranguing check-point scenarios

Disoriented minds on parade
Neglecting the obvious as their palms
Spread for Murtala's head.

But if lucky, you'll meet a few
Good ones; dedicated and straight
But only few, very few.

## THE PRETTY SECRETARY

I know a secretary
Pretty and humane
Calm and kept.
Salutes in motherly ways.
Sure, that is unconnected
To her job.
Our pretty secretary
Is lazy and sluggish; works
At snail speed. Oh, you should see,
Late by default

Nine-to-five turned
Eleven-to-three.
Twelve is break
And she'll have two hours of it

On and on the contractor waited
Napped and turned,
Amid grunts and curses
"Please, sir, you'll come back tomorrow"
-*School runs* call.

## WHOSE FAULT? (I)
*(Electioneering)*

Whose fault is it?
That the ballot papers drank too much and over slept
That some of them grew legs and took a long stroll
That the voting queue grew cold and empty
That the polling officers were hungry and accepted 'kola'
That there are more thumbs for the umbrella
That a party's logo is missing from the ballot paper
That no printer in the land is politically useful
That tribunal members are beaming with smiles

## WHOSE FAULT? (II)
*(Reverse motion)*

False smiles abound.
Faces reflecting our:
Ineptitude
Retro-progress
Gross loss

Masquerade smiles;
Beaming flashes on our:
Yawning gullies on the highway
Pot-bellied potholes dug by pot-bellied masters.

## WHOSE FAULT? (III)
*(for the street kids)*

Once again the street kids
Are calling; a shelter, clothes
On their backs, crumbs from the
Master's table is all they crave.

If mercy shows her face, they
Shall have a doctor,
A good teacher,
A ride on a bus
A trip to the city square
And other merriment

But whose fault is it that these
Are a mirage
For the street kids?
Whose fault?

## WHOSE FAULT? (IV)
*(Finding answers)*

Oh Nigeria!!!
Are we now the little giant?
Our status in jeopardy
Like a dropped bad habit.
Whose fault?
That the dreams of our heroes
Quiver in fear.
Fear of this path we ply
This path of grand-corruption.
Erupting evil beyond comprehension
Our thoughts in constant collision
But panacea seems far away.
For these and more, whose fault?

Who is to blame for these endless sub-committees?
This empty rhetoric party in the upper chamber?
Most say we are charmed against progress.
But, why not break the charms the best way we can-
Restoring our dignity among lands.
Brightening our shamed faces-
Wiping these tears of stunted glory?
Oh, who did this to us?
Who stamped this seal of retrogression
On our palms? Who chiseled our tender buds?
Oh sure, the bastard stunted our laughter;
He suspended our laughter in slow time, while we wait.
In endless sequence.
Like a widow anticipating her husband's homecoming
Like stone about to be cooked. Oh…

No, brothers, this feels like waiting for a dead horse to breathe.
Expecting a song from a dead bird; a goat's bark.
But whose fault?
Whose loin cloth should we hold for this self-sin?
Who is to be grilled?

# WHOSE FAULT? (V)
*(Economics)*

Let's find the knob for food prices
Let's do the same for oil prices
These knobs keep shifting in inches
Ignoring developmental indices

Whose domain is it to fix the zeros
Zeros are at the discretion of the oyibos
These white skins bring inverted favours
Favours that in no time translate to Chaos

Who has the keys to the World Bank?
Our debts keep piling in high ranks
While we befriend the lords of the Bank
Friendship that plunges us deeper in the shank

## BEYOND THESE WALLS

*The distance that separates us*
*These concrete walls do not compensate.*

Cruelty rules in this hate-kingdom;
Behind these bars that barricade us from freedom
Tiny space of near furnace
Chipping our lives bit-by-bit
And halting our dreams.
If you must know, yes, I was a conditional criminal
But no, not the type done in air-conditioned offices
With gold pens, phonetics and signatures.
This is a street tale I must tell, if my kids mustn't feel-
The present *pain* of being Nigerian.
The pain of looking and not seeing;
Of touching and not feeling.
Right before the people's court I was tried.
A crime of meager standing
Though it got me surrounded
By a jungle justice crowd
Their faces like jungle wanderers.

*The distance that separates us*
*These concrete walls do not compensate.*

A dip in *Iya* Tope's frying pan was my crime
A dip for a few *akara* balls, ignoring the hot oil
A fair share of blisters it would be,
But, sure to re-store my empty stomach.

A penalty strung to the crime it could have been.

But the District Police Officer knew better.
My wretched lawyer friend couldn't do any better
A wrenching ride on that rickety van was mine
A wrecking of my right arm and scapular was the
Introductory salute within these walls

*The distance that separate us*
*These concrete walls do not compensate*

The real thieves are nowhere within these walls
Their looting is cheered with accolades
Banners of celebration grace their chambers
Plaques of recognition from groups that grope
Their blind seers lie prostrate
But nemesis awaits them like cancer of the prostrate
Their long convoys bear endless waiting for the masses
Convoys that convey conversations of falsified figures
Con-versations often void of conscience

*The distance that separate us*
*These concrete walls do not compensate.*

The clock never stopped for a moment
I'll be doing some time within these walls
My dreams paused within these walls
Take my words to my people outside these walls
We must invoke the forces of pure justice
This battle we must win holds a fierce process

This battle will bring forth true values
A sure birth of peace,
A sure rebirth of a giant
A new Nigeria born out of these walls.
We can. We will.

# ***WHISPERS OF NATURE***

## WATER NOTE (I)

Don't disrupt the sleep of the sea bed.
No, don't whisper chaotic tunes from
Your farting machines.

The marine gods frown and curse those evil steps
As you approach in coal stained feet and greased palms.
Queen, Mary and Mercy: Giant vessels of ironic
Carnage, tear the sea surface apart. Severance
That leaves tears on the water face.

Surface clad in a billion china pieces like glazed scales of the
Tilapia; Sparkling in splendor, and smiling to the sun.

Don't disrupt the sleep of the sea bed.

Never punctuate its snore with rickety gongs and
Broken terracotta. Never pour tar in its hollow
Nostrils, nor shut its eyes to perpetual closure.
Listen to the unending songs of the water.

# WATER NOTE (II)

The water is well fed with anchors,
Keys and the Captain's poo.
She had enough at war times.

You fed her with heads and limbs;
Not yet digested. More still come like unsolicited
Sacrifices to Orisha Nla.

Enough please!

The skulls of African slaves peep in-between
The sea's dirty teeth. Drums of Colgate would be
Useless.

 The wasted blood of Ayobami, Nnamdi
And Bello killed its purity like blood bags in
The village stream.

The slaves of old are still fettered
In Atlantic chains, rhyming songs of despair as
They watch the earth.

They quiver at slavery's new uniform:
It now wears a bright yellow dress and red hat;
Stained with eternal guilt and suffering

Listen, my errands are not in vain.
These words do not resound:
They are still, steadfast like *Olumo* rock.

## EARTH'S GROAN
*(For Japan)*

Listen, can you feel death's breath-
Beneath these rubbles?  If you can, feel
Once more the cold feet of Takashi and Kitasata
Taking rude steps over your sunken breasts

That loud bang lingered, bringing offspring
Of hate and untold torture: mangling thousands
Amid twisted spines and gaping skulls
As the fireman's boot buries us deeper

On, we searched for Hirobumi and Hara
But saw only photos and crayons
And blood and toes without feet
We now bathe in tears and mud.

Baby Yoritomo has questions for nature
But answers seem in century old loops
To what do we owe this hateful shake?
We turn this debris for answers.

# DUSK...

Dusk buries the sun
In a black cocoon. Quenching
Fierce furnace heat. Halting heat
Of day-long triumph. The moon
Anew from day-long slumber.
Big grin and warm. Peeping
In pious boldness.
Fluid white petals in
Suspended garden above;
Ever pure and static

## WE PELICANS

Virile swerves in quest for bread
Determined dives for the sea's best.
Pouch beneath beak, like a food nest
In white or brown we are bred

Here, we bloom in chill, and warmth-
Same difference. Feathers and plume
Beaks that spell the sea food's doom
Pangs of hunger exhume our wrath

Our obscure language like fond codes
Ferments unity of brown and white
Strengthening efforts of contrite
As we repair cords like the pharma- cod

# SHADOW TALKS

Thin twin of unsolicited trail
Perpetual copycat of my every move
With skin of no texture, feel or gleam
Your lips rattle but no audible conversation
Sometimes I feel we could talk
But a wasted effort that would be
In loneliness you sit with me
But loneliness wears a new look
And never ceases to be loneliness
Becoming a greater form

So lazy you seem
When I am attacked in the streets
You mimic my every punch
But none is felt by "them"
When I'm hit, I feel
And wonder if you feel too.
On that hot Alsatian chase
Did you gasp? Did you share my hurt?
I heard my heartbeat, but not yours
You Cheat!

Do you thirst and hunger?
Do you smell the beer before I gulp?
Or do you gulp with me?
But my 33cl stays 33 in my living pot
So, where's yours?
When my buds jubilate for suya
Do you salivate?
But your growth seems healthy

Sometimes you are taller, fatter.
I repeat: You Cheat!

And you cheat more with my Eve
When I part her branches, you part.
I part in search of knowledge
But you part in search of "Truth"
And truth seems far away.
So far away my thin twin
Men have searched and died
When we search together
It's like a "four some"
Of what use are you to me?

## WASHED ASHORE

How foolish [albeit evading intent]
Your choice of a "mourning" shore?
Heading for a solo voyage: omni function
Needing none aboard your invisible ship.
Faulty compass and anchor of discord.
Yodeling to the unknown; set on auto sail.
The locals query your mission even at your death.
But, food will suffice in lieu of answers.
Blue baby whale of ill fate
Heart as big as a car
Heart and all, now sit in greedy bowels
Cursing your foolish-solo voyage.

# BLACK RAIN

Now it doesn't seem like noon. We stood,
Watching the sun cower; in snail model.
All her hotness gone in a moment like a
Water drop in hot pan: a second in splinters.

Now it doesn't seem calm. We stood,
Watching the unseen brush paint the earth
In circles. Cloudy palette with black ink: ink streams
In a billion rays. A message to earth-a black message

Thunderous message, rummaging within and
Beyond in fierce consciousness…a spiked palm
Petting the earth's back, and pelting us with stones.
A million shields spelt futility as tear streams gushed.

The king's court now at par with the yards
Yawning gaps abound in feted freedom
With metallic romance as we seek calm
And brightness after the black rain.

## OUR SHORTENED HOUSE

Or is it my mind's mystery? How, our brick bungalow
So big; proceeded on a retro trip. Its placid heart led the way
Then, came the shrinking of slow time; an inch a season.

On and on, from a towering height to a towel's length
We sought the strange spade men of this housing trauma
Who perhaps dug at nocturnal halves; tirelessly seeking

A vanishing edifice; our abode so dear and homely. The
Earth men toiled in futility. Sweats in beads of grease and
Blood. So, on we lived, until the cathedral entered the hut.

# ***Living and Hereafter***

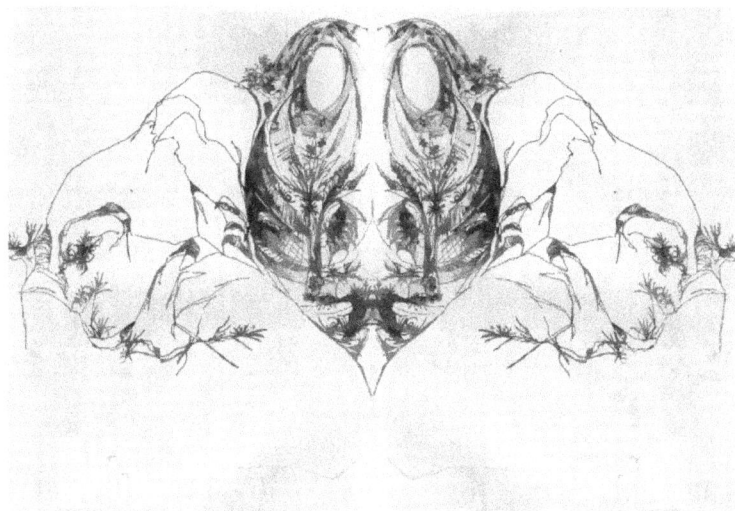

## THIS CLOCK

Didn't we just say it?
Predictable antique on a constant loop. There you are,
Making tickling turns. Pro-cyclic rings of little rest.

Again, if we ask, please don't tell.
The sun plays your role; unending natural timepiece
Slow to burn or lie in faulty sequence.

We just noticed,
You've been on, and on: years and more and some more
Ticking and making unsolicited rounds, forever

## INSOMNIA

Squeaky chips abound: my only companion
In sound form, not an upright buddy.
The night is the Nile, with the depth of the Niger.
It howls darkness as with a thousand horses' might;
Dark darkness, not a twinkle nor aeronautic insects

Feel the malice of your eyelids,
Like the scuffles of the kings' wives;
Regurgitating madness in royalty-Shameless.

Feel the callousness of your eyelashes,
Bearing form as the palace broom; tough with age
And pricking odd points-paths, pots and pubes

Feel the artistry of the shadows
Making silent shows. Clothes and curtains miming
*Iganmu* comes to my room.

Sleep's a hovering deity. She perches at will
No shrine, no priest and no palm oil on cocoyam.
My 'day-night' is on a loop and if I stoop it might stop,
Flowing forth and ushering true night, as the King's
Wives sweep the palace-peacefully.

# CUT ME NOT

Still within the walls of womb,
I see grandma's callous trade.
Shrill cries of Titi and Sisi
Still hurt my unformed ears.
We watched from the land of the unborn.
And prayed to be conceived by humane mothers
On Titi's day, we asked Ogun to seize all metals
But grandma still had her cruel tools.
Her anti-good party obeyed her commands
Each, fueling different stages of the black act
On Sisi's day, we watched in bottled rage.
But, mere rage changed not our plight.
Grandma's callous surgery sailed on
Face emotionless, effortless; "heartless"
Like a skilled Medical General
Blade blazed through
Blood seeped through
Cries of high timbre called
But the gods nodded in unison
So, I'll soon be here.
A baby girl of innocence
And parts of tenderness.
Cut me not when I come
I'll be prudent in mother selection

# FOURTEENTH STEP

Joy and laughter herald my coming
Drums roll, waists twist, muscles ripple
In mad celebration as I enter the world again.
I know these faces. That's Auntie Chioma.
She'll sprinkle holy water on me for the fourteenth time
Father frets and consults; A tragic mix of gods.
But none can make me overstay my fourteenth visit
The mud fireplace is fresh from mama's artistry
The wall patterns are smeared with my finger prints.
I shall stain more this time
Making markings of dust; fuelling feelings of peril.

I am *Nonyenim.*
I am the curator of puffy eyes and wet nose
I am indifferent to wails from the village walls

Your sadness is my joy
Your sorrow drives me further in death's arms.
Your pain I relish, As I take my fourteenth step.

# THE GRAND CHURCH

She sees all
She sees the white
And the black

She sees the traumatic mix
She sees the fakeness of "white"
Even black seems real and upright.

Some whites are true
She likes that, and wants
A changed black.

# BLOODFIELD

Faraway wails,
Grunts and gnashing
Blood fountain overflows
On dry earth,
For a futile fight

The land is "barren"
A hiatus in peace
A broken cord
Of calm
Of solace

The commander's voice
Shatters walls of men;
Fathers of fond memory,
Brothers of passionate bond,
Sons of happy hope

Too many lost
Broad shoulders caress the earth
Welcome the carnival of worms
Eyes roll out from sockets
Heads argue with spines

Femurs marry Fibula
Phalanges marry scapular
In this a marriage of hate,
Of shame,
Of homicide?

# LINGERING LAGER

Smoky spirits smile from ash graves,
Reddened dots of slim sticks that
Caress lips of African *colour*

Lager calls. one, two, three, four…zzz
A thud and I am back. Lager still lingers
Poking pockets and trimming wallets

Welcome to my regimen. Where we worship
Gods of hops and barley and *more*. Where
We sensually sip, and inhale, and puff.

I, you, we gulp in the evening(s)
Asa strums. Soon she becomes two: Asas
Or three in my *clear* vision.

Her guitar strings are 16
No, they are 12
You nitwit, they are 2

Lager spread the thighs
Of my wallet. Cowries
Sprout in their nakedness

But who will judge my judgment
In this righteous gathering of wise fools?
But wait! The lager still lingers.

# OF DROPS AND SMOKE

Roundtable, round swirling smoke
Of unending pipes, and smooth glasses
Let the light monger parade.
Unseen seas and rivers
Turn into oceans of wild dreams
Of flat falls and undulating dunes

Take me, inhale me
I am the smoke
Of nicotine centenary
Sip me, gulp me

Of liquor island
All of me, I'll ripple
In your tummy

Let me take solace in
Your bowel of solitude.
I'll defy biology
Biology of my weird class teacher
The scientist taught me
Wrong. A wrong path he led.

I am African. Of firm
Knowledge and tutelage
My root cures all ailments

## UP NEPA!!!
*(beg for your rights)*

We sat in sad circles
Arms akimbo, our brows knitted.

Sweat ruled the night
Multiple Emperors of mosquitoes

Each, padded landing
Took a quarter of a milliliter

The once swirling
Metal hung still – in endless wait.

Tear trickled down the
Candle. And the coil coiled in anticipated defeat.

Then, dark turned light
Our light ever held behind gates of enigma

Behind gates of figures
3,000Kilowatts wallows in weathered wait

I abhor a carnival of mediocrity,
Of trampled kilo-mega dreams killed on roundtables

But, I'll be merry
For the light turned the metal round and round.

# TITI DON KPAFUKA
*(Poem in Pidgin 1)*

Me, I no understand dis kain thing
She work like Jackie, sotay jaundice embrace
Her. "Titi, bodi no be firewood o", na wetin
I tell her

Day by day, Titi dey pack, push and prune
She dey wash, weave and whine. Even truck
Lazy for wia Titi dey
"Titi, e don do," na wetin I tell her.

Just like river wey dem pour crude oil
Titi begin change colour; black, blue and red.
The thing do like rainbow sometimes.
But I bin tell her.

When time reach, Titi close eyes, she no move
Nor talk. She be like stick for rain; strong kakaraka
I cry sotay, my eyes dry.
"No wori, e go better" be wetin her eyes talk

## TICHAR DEY BLOW GRAMA
*(Poem in Pidgin 2)*

Mr Lexicon get big mouth. Big words like
Olumo Rock dey commot from im mouth
Dim...dim...dim

If you put  ear for ground
You go hear giant oyibo weh dey make
Gbam...gbam...gbam

But, Mr Lexicon pikin na olodo,
Im nor sabi spell anything
At all...at all...at all

## WATERY EYES

Watery eyes
Blind man-rubber bowl.
And watery eyes
Fist capped the wooden staff
Staff smooth and silvery from age
A septuagenarian's support
Aiding wobbling limbs
Stretched; Naira-calling renditions,
Garnished with the pauper's creed
Watery eyes
Blind man-rubber bowl
Led by anchor boy

## GRANNY'S SLUMBER

One last breath; she sleeps forever
Stone still smile she wore whenever
Be merry; sip a shot
In grief and joy, life is short

# CLAPPING PAWS

Cynical leaps on pedestals of power
Tail curls up bundles of Dead Presidents.
Fur strands, with no definite colour.
Are you a chameleon?

A "green cat" – you were meant to be,
With white stripes that inject purity.
But, you heed the counsel of the Old Black Witch.
And, inflict your subjects with Old Black plagues

Your whiskey smeared whiskers twitch at the whiff of Naira
Your stripy muscles ripple at the sight of mice-masses
Your back forbids the earth
But, you lay paws-up on Naira field

Smoking pipe, nodding to sonorous notes.
If you could, you'll have Bach strike the chord for you
But a wish that is, and a wish it'll always be
For the powers of Dead Presidents are limited;

You can't woo the dead to a two man concert

Your paws clap, kittens jeer and cheer
At mundane feats felt by none
You'll soon be gone
To the land of dust

Your paws suspended in dust
Breathless, Lifeless

As you exit the stage
Another role poorly played.

# STRAIGHT MAZE

These men of callous oddity
Rendering notes of blank apathy
In the manner of a dubious chorister
With voice of emptiness and lost timbre

Here, gold crowns sit on mediocrity
In the midst of sages and the nerdy
And youths while and chill on banisters
Oh! what a time to waste my charisma

Let us switch heads like brain charity
Getting rid of the shame and calumny
Sending smiles from Asaba to Niger
And redeeming the pride of Nigeria

This maze seems deep and creepy
With darkness embracing heartily
While calling in command like a father
But we refuse firmly. Now we know better.

## CYCLE

Your birth cry was heard
by the lonely old man.

You take your wife
and work, eat and make love.

Gray knocks. You open with shock
but willingly accept. You hear

More birth cries as a lonely
old man and die[so they say]

## AYESHA

When Ayesha died, she was laid in black pearls and gold rings
When Ayesha died, she wore *Gucci* and rubber hair
When Ayesha died, the city brewery smiled.
We ate and danced and smiled
She wasn't happy. She
Died in debt.
Debt death.
Ayesha is not smiling
Tomorrow her creditors will
Come knocking. We'll ignore the bastards.
Soldier boots and hard sticks beat the door. The *Iroko* will cry.
But Ayesha, isn't smiling. She needs not the pearls and gold rings.

## ESCAPISM

Stealth steps down the steps
An escape from home grown
Chaos. Faking finesse seems
Too difficult. I'll take a street
Run to the madman's cave
Of boxed serenity and convoluted
Dreams. Aha, at last I'll be free.

My mind makes morbid faces at my
Horrible getaway. I feel a back-heart beat;
Rescinding  my plan before fruition. But,
My ears are clad in a rascal cat skin,
Aiding my cat willed dream of a rascal
Fatherhood, and shyness from the cells of
Husbandry.  Aha at last I'll be free.

Rolling notes from a Motorola
I presently detest. And for the vibes
Of the Nokia, I'll toss it in a nook.
All you mad peripherals of technological
Anti-climax. Let me take a lone walk
Down the streets, yodeling and tugging
At my *dada* . Aha at last I'll be free.

What madness it is here? Enveloped in chaotic
Dusts and devilish rants. What metal horses
Farting through long metal orifice, and romancing
Elephants on wheels? Looting bounties of peace
And serenity. Any prize in hooting at will? Oh, look
The General's men strips a damsel; a mixed marsh

Of beauty and madness. Aha at last I'll be free.

Where is my freedom? The breeze seems still
Where are the wings of unbridled passion?
Where are my long legs of seamless treks?
Who holds the keys to the mosquito's mouth?
Who caused the cock to chase the hen fiercely?
Why did the chicken cross the Agbor bridge?
Will I complete my escape from chaos? Will I?

## FIGHTING

Losing hope is fighting with a vehement villain.

# THE SEARCHING SONNET

Who will be my friend?
Beside me in fair tarry
Here to divinely comprehend
Trudging on when seasons vary
Yodeling life's music. You could be distant
But feelings within not withering
In strides; be vale, non hesitant
Some loud chats will keep us smiling
Nightly love fights
Will make our love peak
Surely, that will make me feel right
You bother not. 'Cos my heart is meek
Striving to halt long years of boredom
Be my friend, we'll chart a path of freedom

# ***Haiku***

## WOMAN

HER
Ovaries are fighting
Now, a war of two cities
Bloodbath in-between

BIRTH
Labour "Laws" come tough
Constrictions at intervals
Baby cries, both sleeps

BODY
The architects failed
Angelo could not draw this…
This accurate piece.

# MAN

HIM
Testosterone rage
Slaps of pleasure calms him down
He reloads and shoots

SIMPLE MIND
Interrogation
The straight path's the way to go
Drinks after scuffles

TAKING THE LEAD
Sit behind and watch
Maria holds the new roadmap
We arrive safely

# NATURE

SUN
God's flame from afar
We blink in awesome wonder
She sleeps through the night

RAIN
Sputtering on earth
Our ten storeys become one
The palm bows for you

AIR
He made for malice
Invisible essential
And his will gave in

EARTH
This I always thought
Flat vast flat frying pan flat
The teacher was right

# MIND REVIVAL

STEER THE WHEEL
Live, but for a day
Take the stage and get applause
Ensure smiles at dusk

YOU CAN
The will makes the steps
You unwind in victory
Live well and play well

# FOR SCIENCE

FEAR
The driver's red eye
Smoke came from a vent within
His wheel grew stubborn

CAUTION
Metal threads above
We speak the language of volts
On and off we switched

SKIN DEEP (I)
Ann in John Hopkins
Anaesthetics and some more
Front, now well rounded

SKIN DEEP (II)
Discomfort pushed Dave
Surgeon added more and more
His wife flashed a smile

VOYAGE
Blue and black around
Clear salty splash all over
Captain is naked

# FOR FAMILY

LOVE CASTLE
Walls in great blossom
Colours in warm tete-a-tete
Now, serve the love tea

DAD
Ika Hercules
Let's ensure we get it right
Here come the good works

BIG TREE
Unknown sprouts from stalks
Some make us smile, some cause rage
Grandma's peace dinner

# FASHION MIND 1

THREADS
White, blue, yellow, green
A mad man taught you his style
The queen forbids this

ANOREXIA
Fit, fit foolish dress
Toned femurs on  the runway
Paris detests fat

AFRICA
Aso oke cat walk
Kente fever rocks the town
The west mix is good

# FASHION MIND 2

SEAMSTRESS
Ignore the labels
She makes a piece from pieces
United colors

SINGER
Tender feet dancing
In and out dips the needle
Now, 'adire' smiles

POLKA DOTS
Blue, yellow, green, red
The happiness of colors
This Victorian art

## FASHHION MIND 3

FASHION POLICE
Are they fashion gods?
Waving the wands on runways
Feel fine and be you

ZIPPER
A hard job it is
A notch more, I might just break
Much to hold in place

HER HAT
Straw-hat on the Beach
The sun filters through with ease
Eyes glisten anew

# ADOLESCENCE

TIME
Like flickering light
Changes rather confusing
And then we feel grown

SEASON
Guidance most needed
Their minds rattle this season
Best find a balance

PUSHING
We try anything
Sometimes it could be extreme
Now, our mind's a lab

## BOY-CHILD

PLAY
I should play this way
Maybe dolls aren't so cool
Get Lil' trucks and balls

STYLE
My small Cowboy Hat
Shirt tucked in mini Levis
You should see my boots

LITTLE GENTLEMAN
Respects his sisters
Feel the strength of protection
Always watching Dad

# GIRL-CHILD

CARE
She's all we'll protect
And nurture with great values
Daddy's Lil Princess

TENDERNESS
Gentle ways reflect
These tiny fingers will rule
A nation is born

PLAY
Going beyond dolls
Could have a toy truck, maybe
My mind is not all Barbie

## BABY

ARRIVAL
Must be hard for mum
I think Dad's a soldier too
Bright lights around me

ME
Don't get mad at me
See my cry as laughter too
As first teeth cut gum

AFFECTION
Take me to grandma
I long for that seasoned warmth
Her wrinkles tell tales

# ACTIVITY

DOING
Steady steps onward
A quick pause for appraisal
Now look back and smile

EARNING
A bag of cowries
Sure made full from daily toils
Pieces from your sweat

PAUSE
Feel the wheels turning
Whirl, on and on. Pause and rest
When it's right, whirl on.

# GROWING

SCUFFLES
We can't do without
This difference that build us
Days aren't the same

STEPS
Can't wait to be grown
Now these colors are too bright
Now, I lace my shoes

CHOICES
Many things to try
Like picking tiles from a box
Some burn our fingers

# EMBRACE

FRIENDSHIP
Now drifted apart
Years of fondness set apart
Nostalgia deepens

THE WALK
Feet in unison
Those plans we carefully made
Now under the sand

THE PUSH
A pat on the back
Golden words that spur action
Please keep them coming

# INTERACTIONS

TRUST
And just one spoiled shot
One wrong move that changed it all
Now our backs have turned

BELIEVING
Making the wrongs right
Also making firm our yes
The straight assurance

# COLOR MIX

BLEND
Lovely firm handshake
This firm black and white handshake
Awesome color blend

WELCOME
Your face of coffee
Now welcomes mine that can blush
How I love the mix

SMILE
The lines from your smile
Pretty lines of no color
All I see is warmth